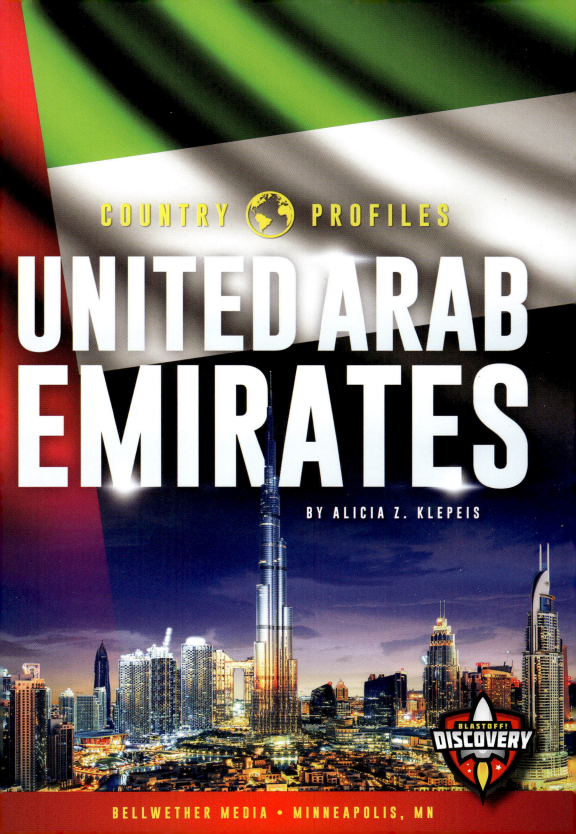

COUNTRY PROFILES

UNITED ARAB EMIRATES

BY ALICIA Z. KLEPEIS

BELLWETHER MEDIA • MINNEAPOLIS, MN

Blastoff! Discovery launches a new mission: reading to learn. Filled with facts and features, each book offers you an exciting new world to explore!

This edition first published in 2023 by Bellwether Media, Inc.

No part of this publication may be reproduced in whole or in part without written permission of the publisher.
For information regarding permission, write to Bellwether Media, Inc., Attention: Permissions Department,
6012 Blue Circle Drive, Minnetonka, MN 55343.

Library of Congress Cataloging-in-Publication Data

Names: Klepeis, Alicia, 1971- author.
Title: United Arab Emirates / by Alicia Z. Klepeis.
Description: Minneapolis, MN : Bellwether Media, Inc., 2023. | Series: Blastoff! discovery. Country profiles | Includes bibliographical references and index. | Audience: Ages 7-13 | Audience: Grades 4-6 | Summary: "Engaging images accompany information about the United Arab Emirates. The combination of high-interest subject matter and narrative text is intended for students in grades 3 through 8"– Provided by publisher.
Identifiers: LCCN 2022050050 (print) | LCCN 2022050051 (ebook) | ISBN 9798886871517 (library binding) | ISBN 9798886872774 (ebook)
Subjects: LCSH: United Arab Emirates–Juvenile literature.
Classification: LCC DS247.T8 K58 2023 (print) | LCC DS247.T8 (ebook) | DDC 953.5704–dc23/eng/20221018
LC record available at https://lccn.loc.gov/2022050050
LC ebook record available at https://lccn.loc.gov/2022050051

Text copyright © 2023 by Bellwether Media, Inc. BLASTOFF! DISCOVERY and associated logos are trademarks and/or registered trademarks of Bellwether Media, Inc.

Editor: Rachael Barnes   Designer: Brittany McIntosh

Printed in the United States of America, North Mankato, MN.

TABLE OF CONTENTS

A DAY IN DUBAI	4
LOCATION	6
LANDSCAPE AND CLIMATE	8
WILDLIFE	10
PEOPLE	12
COMMUNITIES	14
CUSTOMS	16
SCHOOL AND WORK	18
PLAY	20
FOOD	22
CELEBRATIONS	24
TIMELINE	26
UNITED ARAB EMIRATES FACTS	28
GLOSSARY	30
TO LEARN MORE	31
INDEX	32

A DAY IN DUBAI

BURJ KHALIFA ----

The sun is just rising over Dubai. Not far outside the city, a guide leads a family to a hot air balloon. They soon float high above the desert. Gazelles and Arabian oryx run across the sand **dunes** below. After landing, the family goes for a short camel ride, then heads back to the city.

OTHER TOP SITES
- AL WATHBA FOSSIL DUNES
- LOUVRE ABU DHABI
- MANGROVE NATIONAL PARK
- SHEIKH ZAYED GRAND MOSQUE

To avoid the afternoon heat, they shop, eat, and ice skate inside Dubai Mall. Then, the family walks to the Burj Khalifa. From the giant skyscraper's observation deck, they can see the bustling city and the Persian **Gulf**. Welcome to the United Arab Emirates!

LOCATION

The United Arab Emirates, also known as the U.A.E., is a nation in the **Middle East**. It covers an area of 32,278 square miles (83,600 square kilometers). The U.A.E. is made up of seven **emirates**. Abu Dhabi, the country's capital, lies in the north-central region.

Waters from the Persian Gulf lap the nation's northern coast. Oman borders the U.A.E. in two spots along the Musandam **Peninsula**. Waves from the Gulf of Oman wash onto the country's eastern shore. Saudi Arabia is the U.A.E.'s southern and western neighbor.

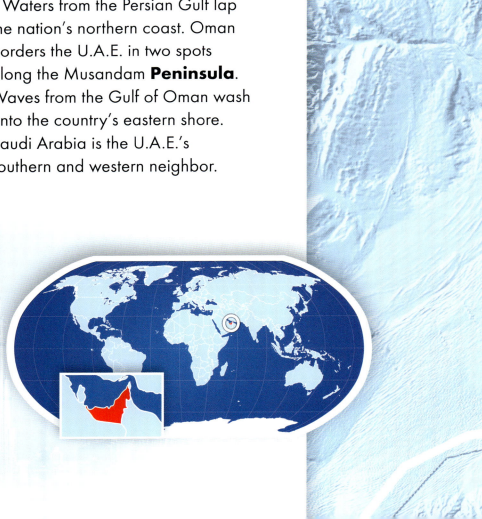

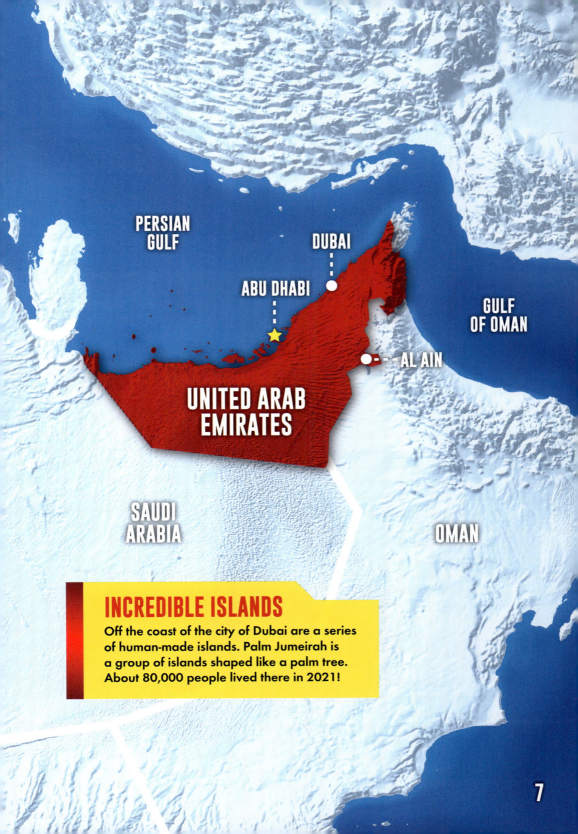

LANDSCAPE AND CLIMATE

Desert covers nearly all of the U.A.E. But green and blue salt lakes brighten the dry landscape near Abu Dhabi. Huge sand dunes constantly shift across the Empty Quarter. A few **oases**, such as Al Ain, dot the desert. The high peaks of the Hajar Mountains rise in the northeast.

= EMPTY QUARTER
= HAJAR MOUNTAINS

EMPTY QUARTER

MAKING IT RAIN

The U.A.E. only gets about 4 inches (102 millimeters) of rain per year. This has led to a lack of freshwater in the country. But scientists are working on ways to get more rain out of overhead clouds!

HAJAR MOUNTAINS

ABU DHABI
Average seasonal highs and lows

JANUARY
HIGH: 73 °F (23 °C)
LOW: 61 °F (16 °C)

APRIL
HIGH: 89 °F (32 °C)
LOW: 73 °F (23 °C)

JULY
HIGH: 103 °F (39 °C)
LOW: 87 °F (31 °C)

OCTOBER
HIGH: 93 °F (34 °C)
LOW: 78 °F (26 °C)

°F = degrees Fahrenheit
°C = degrees Celsius

The U.A.E. is hot and sunny most of the year. Along the coast, the climate is more **humid**. It gets hotter and drier farther south. Temperatures in the desert are often much cooler at night than during the day. Powerful winds called *shamal* blow sand and dust through the U.A.E. every year.

WILDLIFE

Color-changing cuttlefish swim and feed in the **coral reefs** off the U.A.E.'s coast. Hawksbill turtles search for sea sponges as humpback dolphins cut through the waves. In the nation's **mangrove forests**, mottled crabs climb on trees. Flocks of flamingos wade in these forests, eating algae and shrimp.

Sand cats hunt at night in the desert to avoid the fiery daytime sunshine. They seek out rodents and small reptiles. Lesser jerboas are also nocturnal. They hop across the sand in the dark. Arabian oryx roam the desert, seeking out plants to eat.

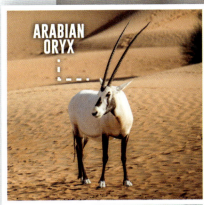
ARABIAN ORYX

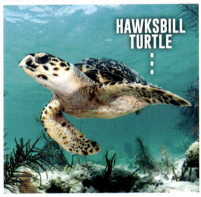
HAWKSBILL TURTLE

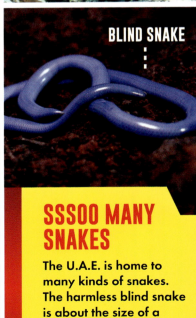
BLIND SNAKE

SSSOO MANY SNAKES

The U.A.E. is home to many kinds of snakes. The harmless blind snake is about the size of a worm. Yellow-bellied sea snakes may come close to shore. They have a deadly bite!

FLAMINGO

10

SAND CAT

SAND CAT

Life Span: about 13 years
Red List Status: least concern

sand cat range =

| LEAST CONCERN | NEAR THREATENED | VULNERABLE | ENDANGERED | CRITICALLY ENDANGERED | EXTINCT IN THE WILD | EXTINCT |

11

PEOPLE

Around 10 million people call the U.A.E. home. Only about 1 million are Emirati. The rest are **immigrants**. Many come from India or other parts of South Asia. Smaller groups of people from Egypt and the Philippines also live in the U.A.E.

Most people in the U.A.E. follow Islam. It is the nation's official religion. Immigrants often practice a religion from their home country, such as Christianity or Hinduism. Arabic is the official language. English is often the common language among people from different countries. Many people in the U.A.E. are **bilingual**.

FAMOUS FACE

Name: Ahlam
Birthday: February 13, 1969
Hometown: Abu Dhabi, United Arab Emirates
Famous for: An *Arab Idol* judge, *The Voice: Ahla Sawt* coach, and award-winning singer known for mixing pop and traditional folk music styles

SPEAK ARABIC

Arabic uses script instead of letters. However, Arabic words can be written with the English alphabet so you can read them.

ENGLISH	ARABIC	HOW TO SAY IT
hello	marhaban	mar-HAB-ah
goodbye	ma'a as-salama	ma ahs-sah-LAH-mah
please (to males)	min fadlak	min FAHD-lehck
please (to females)	min fadlik	min FAHD-lick
thank you	shukran	SHUH-krahn
yes	na'am	NAHM
no	laa	LAH-ah

ABU DHABI

COMMUNITIES

VILLA

Almost 9 out of 10 people in the U.A.E. live in cities and towns. Dubai is the country's biggest city. It is home to around 3 million people. In **urban** areas, people often live in high-rise apartments or large **villas**. Single family homes in suburban communities are becoming more popular. Brick and cement homes are the norm in the countryside. Some have courtyards and gardens where families can relax or entertain.

There are many ways to travel in the U.A.E. Cities often have buses and trains. The nation has an excellent highway system connecting the emirates. Many people drive their own cars to get around.

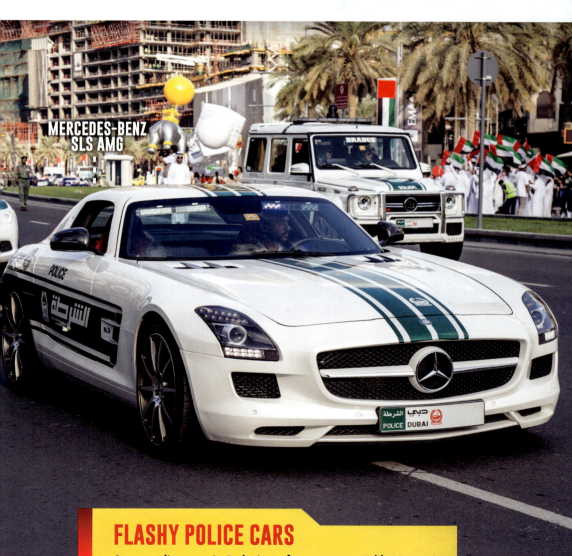

FLASHY POLICE CARS
Some police cars in Dubai are fast sports cars like Ferraris and Lamborghinis. The police have a Bugatti Veyron that can reach 253 miles (407 kilometers) per hour!

CUSTOMS

Folk arts and crafts are an important part of Emirati **culture**. People have been making beautiful pottery for thousands of years. **Bedouin** women use wool for a type of weaving called *al sadu*. They create beautiful items like carpets, blankets, and even camel saddles. **Traditional** *talli* patterns are commonly added to women's clothing.

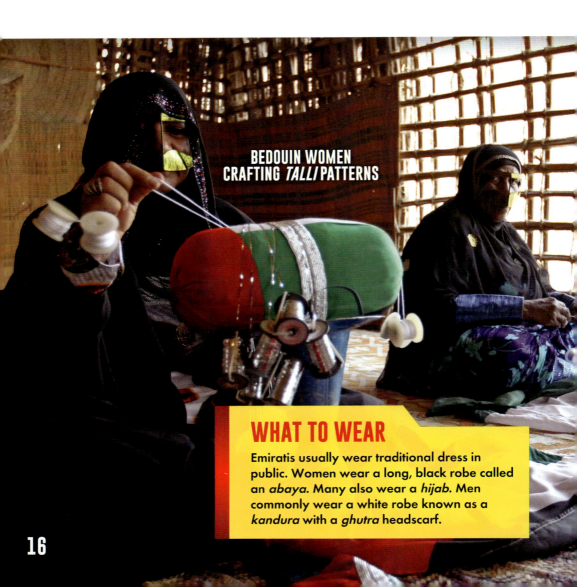

BEDOUIN WOMEN CRAFTING *TALLI* PATTERNS

WHAT TO WEAR

Emiratis usually wear traditional dress in public. Women wear a long, black robe called an *abaya*. Many also wear a *hijab*. Men commonly wear a white robe known as a *kandura* with a *ghutra* headscarf.

AL-AYYALA DANCE

Traditional Emirati musicians often play the oud, a kind of lute. Tambourines and drums are also featured in many traditional songs. Dancers move to the beat of drums in the *Al-Ayyala* "stick dance." This dance uses sticks as swords or spears to share the story of a battle scene.

SCHOOL AND WORK

SCHOOLS AND GENDER

For many years, all public school classes in the U.A.E. were split up by gender. But this is starting to change. In 2018, Grade 1 classes in public schools were mixed. There are now plans to have mixed classes through Grade 4.

Children in the U.A.E. begin school at age 6. Primary school goes through fifth grade. Students learn math, science, social studies, and Arabic. English is often taught as a second language. Many Emirati students attend university. Other students choose to train for jobs in areas such as computer technology, business, or health services.

Over three out of four Emiratis have **service jobs**. Some work in the finance or marketing fields. Others have jobs in hotels, hospitals, or schools. Many people work in the oil and gas business. Factories produce metals, plane parts, and perfumes. Farmers grow dates, tomatoes, eggplants, and cucumbers.

WAITER

PLANE FACTORY WORKER

PLAY

CAMEL RACING

Many people in the U.A.E. enjoy watching sports. Soccer is the most popular. From October to April, camel races attract fans. Some young people enjoy riding ATVs through the desert. Others cruise along coastal waters on boats. Camping in the desert is a fun outdoor activity in the U.A.E. Many families take vacations overseas, often to Europe or eastern Asia.

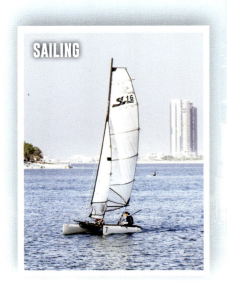

SAILING

Locals and visitors have fun while keeping cool indoors. Shopping and going to the movies are popular pastimes. People visit the Louvre Abu Dhabi museum to see paintings and sculptures from around the globe. Others ski at an indoor resort in Dubai!

INDOOR SKIING

SHADOW SKYSCRAPERS

In 2022, the Burj Khalifa was the tallest building in the world. It is 2,717 feet (828 meters) tall. Design your own skyscraper or create a whole skyline out of cardboard!

What You Need:
- cardboard
- a marker
- scissors
- a bamboo skewer or pencil
- tape
- a lamp
- a blank wall

What You Do:
1. Use a marker to draw the shape of a skyscraper on a piece of cardboard. Be as creative as you wish.
2. Cut out the outline of your skyscraper. Try cutting out some windows to add detail.
3. Tape a bamboo skewer or pencil onto the back of your skyscraper.
4. Place a lamp on a table or the floor. Point it so its light is aimed at the wall. Shut off any other lights in the room. Close the blinds or curtains, too.
5. Turn on the lamp. Hold your skyscraper so that it is between the lamp and the wall. You should be able to see its shadow.
6. Move the skyscraper closer to and farther away from the lamp. How does the shadow on the wall change?
7. You can make more skyscrapers and create a shadow skyline!

FOOD

Breads are popular breakfast foods in the U.A.E. *Khameer* is a puffy roll-like bread. It is flavored with fennel, cardamom, and saffron. *Chabab* is thin and sweet, similar to a pancake. Many Emiratis like *balaleet* for breakfast or dessert. Vermicelli noodles and egg are sweetened with sugar, spices, and rose or orange blossom water.

One of the most popular dishes is *machboos*. This traditional rice dish includes local meat or fish and many spices. *Ouzi* is a favorite Emirati meal of juicy lamb, spiced rice, and nuts. Eating pork is against Islam, so it is unusual to see it served.

MACHBOOS
OUZI

DATE SMOOTHIE

Make this delicious drink for a snack or even breakfast. It is healthy, filling, and quick to make. Have an adult help you make the smoothie!

Ingredients:
1/2 cup dates
2 sliced bananas
1/2 cup plain yogurt
1/2 cup milk
8 ice cubes

Steps:
1. If your dates have pits in them, take them out. Roughly chop the dates into small pieces.
2. Slice the bananas into 1-inch (2.5-centimeter) pieces.
3. Place the dates, bananas, yogurt, milk, and ice cubes into a blender. Blend until the ice cubes are totally crushed.
4. Pour into two glasses. Enjoy!

DELICIOUS DATES

Dates have been part of Emirati food for thousands of years. They are the country's national fruit. They are used in many desserts. One is *luqaimat*, or fried dough balls covered in date syrup.

CELEBRATIONS

The U.A.E. honors many Islamic holidays. They are based on the lunar calendar, so the dates change every year. Muslims celebrate *Hijrī*, the Islamic New Year. People pray and reflect on their lives. They also **fast** during the holy month of Ramadan. *Eid al-Fitr* marks the end of Ramadan. Families gather to feast and give gifts!

December 2 is National Day. This day marks when the U.A.E. became an independent and united nation. Weeks before the holiday, people place red, white, and green decorations on their homes and cars. Parades and fireworks are part of the celebration. Emiratis are proud of their culture!

AL DHAFRA FESTIVAL
The Al Dhafra Festival is a celebration of Bedouin culture. It takes place near the town of Madinat Zayed in the Empty Quarter. Artists display their work, including weavings. Musicians and dancers entertain the crowds. There is even a camel beauty pageant!

TIMELINE

1892
Great Britain takes control of the area's foreign relations, leaving each emirate to govern independently

AROUND 1,000 BCE
One of the world's first systems for moving water to a field of crops is in use at Al Ain

1971
Six emirates join to become the independent U.A.E., with the seventh joining in 1972

1820
Leaders in what is now the U.A.E. work with Great Britain to fight piracy in the area

1976
The nation establishes its first university, the United Arab Emirates University

1958
The first commercial oil discovery is made in the U.A.E.

2006
The U.A.E. holds its first national elections

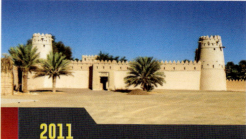

2011
The Cultural Sites of Al Ain, including the famous oasis, become a UNESCO World Heritage Site

2019
Hazzaa al-Mansoori is the first Emirati to travel into space

2010
The Burj Khalifa opens to the public

UNITED ARAB EMIRATES FACTS

Official Name: United Arab Emirates

Flag of the United Arab Emirates: The flag of the U.A.E. has a vertical red rectangle on the left side. The red stands for swords. There are three equal horizontal stripes next to the red rectangle. The top one is green, representing the plains. The middle stripe is white, symbolizing the acts of the people. The bottom black stripe stands for battles. The U.A.E. adopted this flag in 1971.

Area: 32,278 square miles (83,600 square kilometers)
Capital City: Abu Dhabi
Important Cities: Dubai, Al Ain
Population: 9,915,803 (2022 est.)

WHERE PEOPLE LIVE
COUNTRYSIDE 12.5%
CITY 87.5%

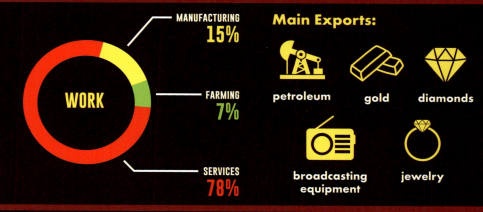

WORK
- MANUFACTURING 15%
- FARMING 7%
- SERVICES 78%

Main Exports: petroleum, gold, diamonds, broadcasting equipment, jewelry

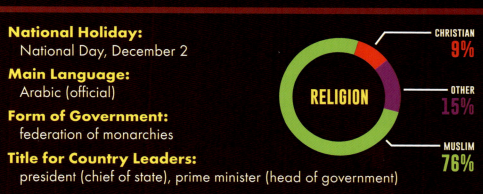

National Holiday:
National Day, December 2

Main Language:
Arabic (official)

Form of Government:
federation of monarchies

Title for Country Leaders:
president (chief of state), prime minister (head of government)

RELIGION
- CHRISTIAN 9%
- OTHER 15%
- MUSLIM 76%

Unit of Money:
Emirati dirham

29

GLOSSARY

Bedouin—the people originally from the U.A.E. and other desert regions of the Middle East and North Africa, many of whom travel continually through this area

bilingual—able to speak two languages

coral reefs—structures made of coral that usually grow in shallow seawater

culture—the beliefs, arts, and ways of life in a place or society

dunes—hills of sand

emirates—states; in the U.A.E. each emirate is ruled by royalty called an emir.

fast—to stop eating all foods or particular foods for a time

gulf—part of an ocean or sea that extends into land

humid—having a lot of moisture in the air

immigrants—people who move to a new country

mangrove forests—thick tropical forests that can grow along coasts in salty swamp water

Middle East—a region of southwestern Asia and northern Africa; this region includes the United Arab Emirates, Egypt, Lebanon, Iran, Iraq, Israel, Saudi Arabia, Syria, and other nearby countries.

oases—green spots in a desert that can support farming

peninsula—a section of land that extends out from a larger piece of land and is almost completely surrounded by water

service jobs—jobs that perform tasks for people or businesses

traditional—related to customs, ideas, or beliefs handed down from one generation to the next

urban—related to cities and city life

villas—large houses or estates with multiple buildings

TO LEARN MORE

AT THE LIBRARY

Goldsworthy, Katie. *Burj Khalifa*. New York, N.Y.: AV2 by Weigl, 2018.

Klepeis, Alicia Z. *Explore Dubai*. Mankato, Minn.: 12-Story Library, 2020.

Spanier, Kristine. *United Arab Emirates*. Minneapolis, Minn.: Jump!, 2022.

ON THE WEB

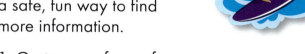

Factsurfer.com gives you a safe, fun way to find more information.

1. Go to www.factsurfer.com.
2. Enter "United Arab Emirates" into the search box and click 🔍.
3. Select your book cover to see a list of related content.

INDEX

Abu Dhabi, 6, 7, 8, 9, 13
activities, 4, 5, 20, 21
Ahlam, 13
Al Ain, 7, 8
Al Dhafra Festival, 24
arts, 16, 17, 21, 24
Burj Khalifa, 4, 5, 21
capital (see Abu Dhabi)
celebrations, 24-25
climate, 8, 9, 10
communities, 14-15
customs, 16-17
Dubai, 4, 5, 7, 14, 15, 21
education, 18
Eid al-Fitr, 24, 25
fast facts, 28-29
food, 22-23, 24
Hijrī, 24
housing, 14
landmarks, 4, 5, 21
landscape, 4, 5, 6, 7, 8-9, 10, 20, 24
language, 13, 18
location, 6-7
music, 17, 24

National Day, 24
people, 12-13, 16, 24
Ramadan, 24
recipe, 23
religion, 13, 23, 24
shadow skyscrapers (activity), 21
size, 6
sports, 20, 21
timeline, 26-27
transportation, 15
wildlife, 4, 10-11
work, 18, 19

The images in this book are reproduced through the courtesy of: Rasto SK, front cover, pp. 4-5; NSThakki, p. 5 (Al Wathba Fossil Dunes); Ingus Kruklitis, p. 5 (Louvre Abu Dhabi); Elena Ska, p. 5 (Mangrove National Park); Kirill Neiezhmakov, p. 5 (Sheikh Zayed Grand Mosque); imageBROKER, p. 8; Aleksandra Tokarz, p. 9 (Hajar Mountains); Marianna Ianovska, p. 9 (Abu Dhabi); Kletr, p. 10 (flamingo); Katiekk, pp. 10 (Arabian oryx), 12, 20 (top); Anita Kainrath, p. 10 (hawksbill turtle); RealityImages, p. 10 (blind snake); Arterra Picture Library/ Alamy, p. 11; Anadolu Agency/ Contributor/ Getty Images, pp. 13 (Ahlam), 24-25; SeaRain, p. 13 (Abu Dhabi); SS 360, p. 14; Frankris, p. 15; marwan naamani/ Alamy, p. 16; Kertu Saarits/ Alamy, pp. 17, 24; Andrea DiCenzo/ Stringer/ Getty Images, p. 18; Yadid Levy/ Alamy, p. 19 (top); REUTERS/ Alamy, p. 19 (bottom); Free_lancer, p. 20 (bottom); Rob Crandall, p. 21 (indoor skiing); vectorlight, p. 21 (Burj Khalifa shadow); Typhoonski, p. 22; Glen Berlin, p. 23 (top);Shakeel Safeek/ Alamy, p. 23 (middle); nblx, p. 23 (bottom); Leonid Andronov, p. 27 (top); Tomasz Czajkowski, p. 27 (bottom); Sergio Delle Vedove/ Alamy, p. 29.